The Withering Petals

By Aesira

In this world, I exist.
But in theirs, I do not.

First published in 2025.

Preface

These poems were written during some of the hardest moments of my life. They are about love, loss, loneliness, and the quiet struggle of trying to stay when everything feels too heavy to carry. I did not write them to perform pain. I wrote them because I needed somewhere to put it.

If you have ever felt invisible, unloved, or like too much and never enough at the same time, I hope you find something in these pages that makes you feel less alone. That is all this book has ever wanted to be.

Acknowledgments

To my friends, who stood by me during the times that inspired these words. You knew when to speak and when to simply be there, and that made all the difference. This book exists because of the strength you helped me find.

To every reader who picks up this book, I hope it reaches you at the right moment and reminds you that your feelings are valid, your pain is real, and you are not alone.

Author's Note

This collection was written across different emotional distances. Some poems came from moments of unrest, others from the quiet that followed. They are not arranged to offer solutions or closure.

Trigger Warning: This book contains themes of emotional pain, self-harm, suicidal ideation, loneliness, and difficult relationships. Readers are encouraged to take breaks, skip pages, or return at another time if needed. If any of these topics affect you personally, please reach out to a trusted person or mental health professional.

This collection is not about healing quickly. It is about noticing what it takes to still be here.

Aesira

1. The World That Isn't

How strange it is
To stand among the living,
Yet feel like a shadow, unseen.

I have built a world of my own,
But is it a curse or my escape?
I see things they cannot,
I talk to walls when I can’t sleep.

They say
something is wrong with me,
but wasn’t it you
who made me this way?

What I was denied in reality,
I shaped with my own hands.
A family, a love, a place to belong.

Even if I know it's not real,
It still feels warmer than the cold outside.

Here, I am held without hesitation,
spoken to without doubt,
seen without question.

In this world, I exist.
But in theirs, I do not.

2. Mistake

I stand accused of something I never did,
Shouted down, ridiculed,
As if I were the one to blame.

How can I defend myself
When I can't read your mind?

Why should I know
what you never told me,
What you never gave me
the chance to see?

You throw words like stones,
Expecting me to guess the unspoken,
To fix the silence you left behind,
But I'm not a mind-reader.

I'm just a person,
Trying to be enough
in a world that won't let me be.
You demand things I can't give,
Promises I didn't make.

And when I fail,
It's me who bears the weight of your anger,
The sharpness of your disappointment.

Why am I the one to blame
When I never knew the rules of this game?

When I look for love from you,
I find only stone,
Cold and unyielding.

Making me question,
Why didn't you let me go before?
If you never wanted me here,
Why did you let me live?

3. Optional

I don't want to be here like this.
I want the feeling to stop,
to fade the way a dream does
when morning comes.

I feel like a shadow,
seen, but never held.
Like I exist and don't,
at the same time.

I answer when they call my name.
I reply when they speak.
I show up, I nod, I stay.
So why do I still feel transparent?

Why does my presence feel optional?
Why do I start to disappear
the moment I'm not needed?

I don’t want to vanish.
I just don’t want to live
as something forgettable,
a background role
no one notices once the scene moves on.

I want to matter
without having to prove it.

4. Unchosen

I keep handing out pieces of my heart
like maybe someone will finally keep one,
but they always fall to the floor
too soft, too heavy, too much.

They say, *"Just friends."*
Like it's a kindness.
Like my wanting is a burden
they need to gently decline.

I tell myself not to ask,
not to need,
not to hope,
but I still do.

Hope, like a fool,
like a child
trying to grow flowers in frost.

But,
There was someone else,
there's always someone else.

Better.
Brighter.
Less Broken

And I sit quietly in the shadows,
wondering what I lack
that love keeps passing me by.

Am I forgettable?
Replaceable?
Am I just a place people rest
until they find where they truly want to be?

I try to believe I matter.
I try to believe I'm not unlovable.
But silence echoes louder than reassurance,
and I'm tired of being the one who waits
and never gets chosen.

5. The Weight of Never Enough

I have stood at the edge,
toes curled on the brink,
felt the wind whisper secrets
I dare not think.

Hands traced cold steel
in a moment of doubt,
a silent scream
I couldn't let out.

I have given,
poured,
broken,
bled.

Held my breath
through words unsaid.

You say I never think of you,
yet my years are ghosts that prove untrue

Your wants, your wounds,
your endless cries.
But what of mine?
Do they not rise?

When did I last hold
something real,
something that was mine to feel?

I am tired
of being shaped and torn,
of chasing love
that leaves me worn.

Not like this.
Not tonight.
I won't be a whisper fading in the light.

I will be the voice I was never given.
I will be the soul that stays unwritten.

6. Echoes in the Dark

Loneliness clings to me,
A shadow that never fades.
I know I exist, but still,
Why am I left in this endless haze?

I reach,
I stretch,
my voice unheard,
But silence is all that returns.

Their coldness burns
where warmth should be,
And in this darkness,
I yearn.

I breathe,
but the air chokes me tight,
The light stabs deeper than night.
Where can I go,
where do I hide,
When no place feels safe to reside?

I have no home,
no refuge,
no care.

Why won't you see me,
why won't you share?

I stand here,
lost,
forgotten in the strife,
I have no home left,
why won't you just take my life?

7. When Rage Becomes Me

There's fire in my eyes,
but my blood runs cold.
This isn't a feeling anymore.
It's who I've become.
It takes up all the space.

The world keeps pushing me to the edge,
or maybe I've learned how to be sharp.
I can't tell if I'm the one bleeding
or the one leaving marks on everyone else.

I curse the world for all it takes,
then blame it when it curses me back.
I keep spinning in the same place,
heat and fracture, over and over.

What am I doing?
Why am I still at war?

My fists are tired.
My voice is worn out.

I don't want to be good.
I don't want to be calm.
I just want this anger
to stop feeling like home.

8. Trapped in the Silence

I wanted to break free,
but here I am,
still stuck in this cage,
I wanted to feel connected,
but I'm just away.

There's this weight in my chest,
a pain I can't touch,
growing, suffocating,
and I can't talk about it.

I'm standing in the middle of a crowd
and still,
I feel invisible.

I see their faces,
I hear their laughter,
I watch their tears,
but it's all just a blur.

The emptiness inside me
that swallows everything.

I'm drowning,
drowning in the silence I can't escape.

The hurt is endless,
the loneliness never leaves,
and the more I try to push it down,
the harder it pulls.

9. Why Love Felt Like a Crime

Why do you make love feel like a crime?
Do you enjoy watching me break,
watching the tears run down my face?

Or is this revenge
for what I did to him,
for the mistakes I can't undo?

You punish me with indifference,
with distance sharp as steel.

Was our bond ever real,
or just a lie I held too close?

You made me believe I mattered,
and then pushed me off the edge.
You were meant to be my shelter,
yet it was your hands
That taught me how easily safety slips.

If you hated my love so much,
why didn't you turn me away at the start?

Why let me believe it was safe to care,
only to strip me bare,
to make me doubt
even the right to stay?

You'll say I'm wrong,
and maybe I am.
Maybe this is my hurt
trying to name itself.

I don't know where you end
and my fear begins.

I only know
love shouldn't feel like this,
and neither should leaving.

10. Not Because You Left

Why do you pretend to care,
say soft things
with a smile that belonged to everyone?

You're kind to everyone
and I mistook that as something more.
Kinship.
Maybe even safety.
But it was nothing.
Not to you.

That's on me though
You were always like this
open palms, closed doors.
I was the one
who hoped wrong.

And now it hurts.
Not because you left.
You didn't.

I just realized
you never cared as much.

Because I thought
I mattered.
Thought it meant something
the way you spoke,
the way you stayed.

But staying isn't the same as caring.
And I see that now.

I built stories
from your polite kindness.
Held onto crumbs
and called it closeness.

I do that a lot
get burned
by my own expectations.

It’s not your fault.
It never was.

I just wanted too much
from someone
who never cared enough.

11. Familiar Misery

It's strange how you push people away
and then blame them for leaving.

You blame them for not reaching out
when you never try yourself.
You test love again and again,
then act surprised
when people finally walk away.

And then you write poems
about how much they hurt you.
But did you ever stop to think
they were hurting too?

Just because you didn't see it
doesn't mean they weren't breaking.
Just because they didn't love you
the way you wanted
doesn't mean they didn't care.

I did.
And I know others who did as well.

But you can't see past your own pain.

That's why you stay stuck in it.
That's why misery feels familiar.

That's why you keep calling it
your only friend.

12. Hollow Kindness

I am a curse
to the ones I love
and the ones who dare
to love me back.

I tried to fix you
when I couldn't even gather
the pieces of myself.
Held you together
while I fell apart
quietly.

I became someone
I don't recognize
trying to make it hurt less
for everyone else.

Maybe that's the joke.
That in trying so hard
to be kind,
to be good,
I ended up being cruel to myself.

No one asks
how hollow kindness can be.

But I don't regret meeting you.
Even when I failed.

If you hurt, I'm sorry.
If my love felt like a wound,
I swear
I didn't mean to bleed on you.

13. I Never Wanted to Break You

I told you
I didn't love you when we met.
If my words and my warmth
said otherwise,
I am sorry.

I hurt the ones who love me.
I ruin the ones I love.
You were no different.
Neither was he.

He stayed
when I had one foot in hell.
You said you loved me
and then disappeared.

How do you hate
the one who kept me alive?
You say you are unloved,
but you had people.
A place to belong.
I never did.

He made me feel
like I mattered.

You said I was your home.
But he was mine.

I tried to open myself to you,
but you didn't know
how to hold what I gave.

That's when I knew
I could never stay.

So don't blame him.
If someone is at fault,
let it be me.
For being too broken,
too slow to heal.

For hurting
the person I never meant
to break.

14. Dear Tyler

I don't know how to fix you.
I don't even know how to hold you
without breaking too.

But I wish you saw what I see.
Not the cracks,
Or the mess
but the fight in your chest
that still wants to believe.

You say you're unlovable.
I say you've just been handed love
in all the wrong ways.
Love that walks out.
Love that lies.
Love that hurts
and turns away at your cries.

You think you're hard to love
but I think you just learned
to expect the leaving
before they even stay.

I won’t promise I’ll save you.
I’m not a cure,
and you’re not a disease.

But if you ever fall again,
I’ll sit with you in the wreckage.
just to remind you,
you still exist.

15. Staying Would Have Hurt More

Sometimes you leave people
to protect them from yourself.
You take on the role of the villain,
so they don't have to.

But I still wonder,
would it have been kinder to stay
and hurt you later?
To let you fall harder,
instead of pulling away when I did?

Love scared me.
Your feelings scared me more.
Because I knew
I couldn't meet them where they were.

And how could I have stayed,
knowing I would never be able
to give you what you deserved?

9 789357 778534

Printed at Repro India Ltd.